MY RUSSIAN ODYSSEY

By

Peter Hill R.D.*

First published in 2023

Copyright © 2023 Peter Hill

All rights reserved

Produced by My Saga (www.my-saga.com)

The right of Peter Hill to be identified as the author of this work has been asserted in accordance with Section 77 of the Copyright, Designs and Patents Act 1988. No part of this publication may be copied, reproduced, stored in a retrieval system, or transmitted, in any form or by any means, without the prior permission of Peter Hill, nor be otherwise circulated in any form of binding or cover other than that in which it is published and without a similar condition being imposed on the subsequent purchaser.

ISBN: 9798394092916

Author

The author at 85

Peter Hill comes from North Lincolnshire. He went to school at Christ's Hospital (the Bluecoat School) and won a state scholarship and an Open Exhibition in Classics to Trinity Hall, Cambridge. Before going up he served two years of national service in the Royal Navy, part of it in London at a military section of the School of Slavonic and East European Studies. He learned Russian to interpreter standard. After Cambridge he joined the BBC as a General Trainee and spent nearly all his career at Westminster as a correspondent and presenter of political programmes such as "Yesterday in Parliament." He also continued in the Royal Naval Reserve for 27 years as a Russian interpreter and was awarded the R.D. and clasp.

After early retirement from the BBC staff, he continued translating and interpreting for businessmen, which took him to Moscow, Hong Kong and Hanoi.

Now in genuine retirement, he paints, learns Italian, plays bridge, walks the dog, and is a National Trust room guide at Petworth House in Sussex.

Contents:

Author	3
Contents:	v
Acknowledgements	i
Chapter 1: The Barfly	1
Chapter 2: National Service	2
Chapter 3: Frinton	18
Chapter 4: Cambridge to Moscow	20
Chapter 5: Diplomatic Ping pong	26
Chapter 6: Reserve Training	27
Chapter 7: Falklands 1982	28
Chapter 8: With Devonshire in Leningrad	30
Chapter 9: Weekend Exercise	35
Chapter 10: Helping an Architect	36
Chapter 11: Ian Trethowan	38
Chapter 12: Moscow and Georgia	40
Chapter 13: Gerald Carroll	45
Chapter 14: Christopher Stephenson	48
Chapter 15: Sailing through Russia	54
Chapter 16: Conclusion	60
Bibliography and sources	62

Acknowledgements

I would like to thank a number of people who have helped me with their memory, or with their correct knowledge of naval terms, or who have read the manuscript to spot errors. They are: Robert Avery, Nigel Hawkins, Aubone Pyke, David Talks, and Peter Hancock. Some of the text has already appeared in Frinton Society newsletters, or been broadcast on 'From Our Own Correspondent'. I owe a lot to the fine teachers of Russian I have had over the years, notably Brian Hawkins, Roy Hurst and Robert Avery. And I owe a lot to my many Frinton friends, and to the Royal Navy.

Chapter 1: The Barfly

BBC TV Publicity still of the author, early 1970s

Sometime in the 1970s, while working as a BBC political correspondent at the Commons, I went into the Press Gallery bar. A well-known barfly from the Press Association looked up from his Guinness and, after a brief exchange, asked me, "Is the BBC the only organisation you work for?"

What could he mean? Did he think that somehow I was spying on, or reporting on, fellow journalists? I suppose he knew that I spoke good Russian. He might even have heard that I disappeared each summer for a fortnight to go back to the Navy. He might also have known, though I doubt it, that I had visited Russia a number of times. But a spy? Ridiculous. Whatever I said to him – and I probably asserted that I was just a Russian linguist – I doubt if he would have been convinced.

So was I a spy – or wasn't I? This is the story of my journey.

Chapter 2: National Service

At school I knew nothing of Russian. At the age of eleven I went off from my home town of Scunthorpe in Lincolnshire to the faraway school of Christ's Hospital near Horsham in West Sussex. I was joined there a year or two later by my brother David. We wore a uniform worn by Bluecoat boys for 400 years.

Bluecoat boy, the author with his brother, David, c 1955

We studied Latin, we studied Greek, and in some cases either French or

German. Even, in my last year, Italian. But Russian was never on the menu. In geography we never studied eastern Europe. In literature we never read Tolstoy or Pushkin. In history, we never studied the Tsars, or the Russian revolution. The only connection with Russia I recall was when I was around fifteen, someone rushed into the Science class and said "Stalin is dead!". But my Russian odyssey only began in my final year. And it began in the well-named Oddfellows' Hall in Brighton. I went there in the summer of 1956. I had gained a scholarship in classics to Cambridge University. But like all British boys (except for those from Northern Ireland) I had to do my National Service first.

The majority of us went into the army, but I did not want to do drill and wear khaki – I had had enough experience of that in the school Combined Cadet Corps every Friday. I wanted to join the Navy, but I soon discovered that this was a privilege granted to few, and candidates had to have 20/20 vision for scanning marine horizons, which I did not.

However, the recruiters in the Oddfellows Hall looked at my record and noted that I had a command of Latin and Greek, and to some extent, French. They told me that the Navy was looking for linguists to train up in Russian. How would I like that? Very much, I said. At the time, I did not realise that this would mean hardly any drill, that I would be wearing plain clothes, and that I would be spending a year at university. And so began my lifelong love-hate relationship with Russian and Russia.

Portsmouth

Royal Naval Barracks, Portsmouth was a desolate place, a cheerless place, a parade ground surrounded by dormitories, washhouses and the NAAFI. In the barrack block to which I was allocated, beds went two by two, one above the other. I got an upper berth with an undertaker's assistant below me. The barracks seemed to be run by bullying Petty Officers (P.Os.) and chiefs. They enjoyed getting us up. "Wakey wakey! Rise and Shine! The morning's fine! You've had your time!! Hands off cocks! On Socks!"

We were issued with the matelot's clothing kit, which included two white round hats (one for best) that bore the 'HMS *Victory*' cap tally (later to become 'HMS *Cochrane*', then 'HMS *President*'), a large square collar with three white bands, a dark blue jumper that pulled over the head, bell-bottom trousers with horizontal pleats and a front flap instead of fly

CHAPTER TWO: NATIONAL SERVICE

buttons, black boots, a white lanyard, a 'pusser's dirk' (which I still have) and the essential Housewife, pronounced 'hussif', a cloth roll with darning needles, cotton, and all that was necessary for 'make do and mend'.

Able Seaman Hill after joining RN at Royal Naval Barracks, Portsmouth, October 1956

At sea you were responsible for maintaining your own kit. We were also provided with a set of 'No.8s', which were lighter blue cotton work clothes, and a kitbag. The final item was a good quality dark raincoat known as a 'Burberry'. Some regulars had them adapted with extra inside pockets to

CHAPTER TWO: NATIONAL SERVICE

store the free ration of Royal Navy cigarettes (600 a month, I seem to remember). The men would take the cigarettes 'ashore', that is, out of the barracks gates and into the Portsmouth pubs, where they could be sold for considerable gain. It was frowned upon for any non-smokers to refuse their ration: it could always be sold on at a discount.

One of the morning lessons was devoted to gas attacks. We were told how to distinguish mustard gas from other forms of gas by their smell. If you smelled any of them, you had to shout, "Gas! Gas! Gas!". If anything got on your skin, you had to rush to the decontamination showers. We were told if we were attacked by nerve gas, there was no smell, and we would be dead within seconds. Who would have thought that a nerve agent was to be deployed over sixty years later in a Southern English town? And then came the practical. We were made to run in our gas masks through a brick tunnel full of tear gas. Having survived that, we were made to repeat the run with our masks off. We all came out coughing, choking and weeping, and took the lesson to heart. I was reminded of that morning many years later in July, 1970, when tear gas was thrown into the Commons chamber. Having beat a hasty retreat, we reporters had to return to the Press Gallery to report proceedings, if only briefly. It was not pleasant. The C.P.O. giving us the gas lessons was once asked by a novice if we could have a window open, as it was rather stuffy. "Look, lad," was the reply, "there's only one place for fresh air – outside!"

Another nerve-shattering day was a visit to HMS *Phoenix*. We were taught how to put out fires at sea, how to distinguish between oil fires, electrical fires and wood fires, and when and how to apply foam, water or CO2. Handling large fire hoses needed strength and teamwork. However, the worst experience was being put in a mock-up submarine, which was then slowly flooded, while we were supposed to string up emergency lighting. How we got out of this claustrophobic nightmare I do not recall, but it is not something I ever wanted to do again. Bayonet drill was pretty scary, too. We had to run at sacks of sand suspended from a pole, shouting, and ram our bayonets into the sack. The autumn of 1956 was the time of the Hungarian revolution and the Suez invasion. One P.O. shouted at us, "You'd better get it right, because you'll be sticking it in a Gippo next week!"

The worst kind of drill was at Whale Island, the Navy's gunnery school noted for its discipline, where the parade ground was not asphalt but loose chippings. Marching on this was very difficult, and it was even worse if you made a mistake. You would be punished by one of the strutting instructors: a circuit of the parade ground at the run, holding your rifle above your head with both hands. The senior man in our little squad was Michael McDonald, who later became a Professor of Islamic Studies in Edinburgh, but he was too gentle for the gunnery instructor (GI) in charge. His efforts were mocked in a loud voice. GIs were the only non-commissioned officers, who were addressed as 'Sir'.

All this was intended to make us useful sailors, whatever our speciality. We were of very mixed ability, social class, education, and physical attributes. One memorable day after joining up, we were ordered to go to the medical section and strip off. We stood in a line, naked, and waited to be inoculated. No-one asked for our consent, enquired about allergies, or explained what was being put in us. No-one had the nerve to ask. But the man in front of me, who was very large, took one look at the hypodermic needle and fainted.

Our so-called basic training ended soon enough, and I was sent to HMS *Mercury* near Petersfield, (a training centre for signal communications) in a large park, to await the next draft for the Russian course. After a short wait, I took a long train journey up to Scotland, then another train out along the coast of Fife, to the small fishing village of Crail.

Crail: Learning Russian

In those days, Crail was far from being the bijou holiday resort it has now become. At that time, it was a huddle of stone houses around a small harbour, whose only attraction for us was the Juke Box Café, where you could hear Elvis's latest hits on the machine, and perhaps engage a local girl in conversation. The other gathering point was the bus stop for St Andrew's, ten miles away, where there were girls a-plenty at the university, and lots of pubs that were open on weekdays.

The camp itself was a good walk from the village. At the guardhouse, past the community hall, you went up the hill to the barrack rooms, which were clustered round the drill square (they were later converted to a pig farm). There was a dining room, a NAAFI, and some admin buildings. Down at the bottom of the hill, which we marched down every day, and across the road, was an airfield. This had been used by the Black Watch and by the Fleet Air Arm in wartime. The central buildings here had been converted

CHAPTER TWO: NATIONAL SERVICE

into classrooms. It was here that their Lordships in their wisdom had moved the Joint Service School for Linguists (or J.S.S.L) from Bodmin Moor.

The camp was run by the Army, but the much smaller naval contingent, each with the rank of 'Coder Special', came under the splendid Commander Maitland-Makgill-Crichton DSC DSO. He was a war hero and an outstanding linguist, formerly known to his men as "Champagne Charlie", and regarded with affection by the *kursanti* under his command. Russian was taught by a wonderful collection of emigré Russians, Ukrainians, Poles, Serbs, and Eastern Europeans, some of them Princes or Counts, still with Tsarist accents, some of them former prisoners – all with great stories to tell. 57 instructors (including some British ones) are listed in a personal memoir by one of the best teachers there was, Brian Hawkins. They included Mr Mandra-Methusaleh, Mr Oljhovikov, Mr Rathfelders, Mr Wolkowinski, Mrs Kravchenko, and the unforgettable Dimitri Makaroff, the producer of some outstanding dramas. It has occurred to me that the electoral roll for the village of Crail must have had more Ivan Ivanoviches on it than McTavishes.

They encouraged us to live a cultural life as well as linguistic training: there was music, choral singing of Russian folk songs, (gathered together in a song book called *Samovar);* there was a regular camp magazine, of the same name, with some surprising contents, such as the war-time memoirs of M-M-C, in Russian (these I donated to the Slavonic section of the British Library). There were also plays - *Hamlet, Othello*, the *Bed Bug*, and others, all in Russian, performed by students who were to become star names on the stage. Jeffrey Wickham was one, who later became President of Equity. On earlier courses there had been Mark Frankland, Denis Potter, Jeremy Wolfenden, Alan Bennett, Michael Frayn, John Drummond and six or more British ambassadors - and on my own course there were Nicholas Slater, the nephew of Boris Pasternak, Peter Carson, former head boy at Eton who became head of Penguin Books, Peter Oppenheimer, Professor of Economics at Christchurch, Oxford, and Rick Pollock, Professor of Russian, who became Mrs Thatcher's interpreter with Mr Gorbachev. Another, who became a close friend of mine, was Harry Eastwood, who already had a first in Russian at Manchester University before he joined up. So, it was a bit daunting to be in this kind of company when I did not even know the Russian alphabet.

However, thanks to the kind Mr Ancipovich and others, I slowly caught up. One of the first lessons I attended was with Mr Henryk Malhomme de la Roche, who was smoking, using a long cigarette holder. He told us that by the end of the lesson we would all be able to speak Russian. First, he waved his cigarette at us and asked, *"Kurite li vi? ('Do you smoke?')"*, to which one answered, *"Da"* or *"Nyet"* as the case may be. He went round the class and then asked a second question: *"Gdye vi zhivyote? (Where do you live?')"*, to which one replied, *"London"* or perhaps *"Edinburgh"* or in my case *"Scunthorpe"*. He came to the last student in the class, a Welsh boy. He waved his cigarette at him and asked *"Kurite li vi?"* After some thought, the answer came. *"Bridgend, sir!"*

After two or three months of intensive lessons and much homework, we took a big exam. We were ranked in order, and then the top twenty naval students went one by one before an Admiralty Board, which consisted of nearly half a dozen senior naval officers and much gold braid. There was also a member of the teaching staff. This board was not so much a test of linguistic ability as of OLQs – officer-like qualities. What school did you go to? Have you any relatives in the Navy? Have you captained a sports team? (Fortunately for me the answer to the last question was 'yes'). There must have been several academic tussles behind the scenes, as some public schoolboys (one with fine manners and a distinguished father in the Navy) were preferred for commissions over far better linguists. Frank Knowles was among those who were not selected, and he later went on to become Emeritus Professor of Modern Languages, and Senior Vice-Chancellor at Aston University. Perhaps it was his accent.

SSEES London: More Russian

So, early in 1957, promoted to the rank of Acting Petty Officer, those of us who had passed the Admiralty Board took the train down to London, and found ourselves billeted in a large former hotel in the heart of Kensington: Furse House, in Queen's Gate Terrace. It was a Wrennery – strictly segregated. Wrens (those in the Women's Royal Naval Service) working at the Admiralty lived in the other half of the building. But no fraternising was allowed. The great advantage of being there was that we changed into civvies, and unless we were the duty officer for the day, we stayed in civvies.

I shared a 'cabin' on the fifth floor with two friends. Each day we would walk down Gloucester Road to the tube station and take the Piccadilly line to Russell Square. It was there, at no. 47, that we learned our more advanced Russian, and did our 'orientation', that is, learned all the technical terms for warships, torpedoes, missiles, mines and the like. We didn't see much of the Navy itself; we had occasional visits to ships and submarines to learn the terminology. On one visit, I was given a sharp reminder in the wardroom of a frigate. I asked an officer if they ever opened the portholes. "We call them scuttles", was the frosty reply. So we had to try to keep in touch with both the Royal Navy and the Soviet Navy, whilst increasing our fluency in the language.

All in all, in the late fifties, around 500 *kursanti* studied in London, under the aegis of the School of Slavonic and East European Studies. Most of them were in the RN – the Army and RAF men were sent off to learn at Cambridge. As part of the centenary of SSEES, Prof. Faith Wigzell wrote a scholarly and well-researched article about those years, roughly from 1952 to 1960. Those of us who did the courses had little contact with SSEES, its canteens, common rooms or students. We mostly ate in the Air Ministry canteen in High Holborn or snacked at the food stall in Russell Square. We were taught by another extraordinary mixture of emigrés: Mr Khruschev, Mrs Cholerton, Madame Alkhazova, Mr Melechowicz, Miss Gavrilovich, Miss Volossevich, Mrs Ivanova and Mrs Knupfer – and those are only the ones I remember. Miss Gavrilovich (whose photograph appeared in Prof. Wigzell's article) was a glamorous young Serb; Mr Melechowicz was a Pole, whose forearms had been blown off, but who bravely managed his chalk with two prongs on his right arm and a leather covered prosthetic fist on the left; Madame Alkhazova was a grande dame from Moldova; and Mrs Cholerton was the Russian wife of the former Moscow Correspondent of the *Daily Telegraph*. I once asked her if she was related to the renowned Mr Cholerton. "Yes, I was", she replied. "Oh really," I perked up, "in what way?" "He was my husband". They taught the conversation and the reading, though often they spoke an old-fashioned, even Tsarist Russian, without the modern colloquialisms, and the books we had to read – modern Soviet novels like Simonov's *Dni I Nochi* about the siege of Stalingrad – were an attempt to stay in touch with Soviet idioms.

Ronald Hingley was the first course director – a man with a 'fractious' relationship with the Director of SSEES, Dr George Bolsover - who drove his charges hard. He wanted to produce modern military interpreters, not

CHAPTER TWO: NATIONAL SERVICE

enlightened lovers of Russian literature and culture, as he imagined Prof. Elizabeth Hill was encouraging at Cambridge. There was considerable rivalry between London and Cambridge, though this was not known to us students, and the rival teaching methods could not really be settled by the marks in the final CSC exam. Many *kursanti* gained very high marks – three on my course got over 80% and were declared "First Class Interpreters". And that was not just because we had to learn between 20 and 100 new words a night, and sit tests every two weeks on pain of expulsion. Hingley was replaced by an even fiercer director, Bryan Toms, who taught grammar and vocabulary with an intensity rarely seen in a university. But then, as one course member was told, we weren't students: "Every lesson is a parade". I recall once when told by Toms that a Russian word meant 'hominy grits', I asked him what they were. He exploded: "I'm here to teach you Russian, not English!". It is even said that Toms took his little red Russian dictionary with him on his honeymoon as he hadn't finished reading it to the end!

In a scholarly paper ('A Special Generation of Speakers of Russian'), Professor Michael Lee wrote : "What was remarkable about both the wartime arrangements and the Joint Services School was the intensity of the training. No school or university either before or since has been so exacting on its pupils."

The living quarters for the early courses (which ran by letters from A to T, and usually each had around 25 members) was 8 Sussex Square, reputed to be a former brothel, where occasional night visitors would ask for 'Big Bertha'. The naval C.O. was Lt. Cdr M. Lukas DSC, who had fought with the Polish Navy.

In 1954 came the move to Furse House. Once, I recall that a bunch of us in our naval-issue civvies were coming up in the deep lift at Gloucester Road tube with a couple of Russians, who were obviously from the Embassy. They talked audibly. As they got out they got a shock when one of us remarked, "*Ochen interesno!*"

On another occasion we were visited at our quarters by police, asking if we had been at the tube station the previous night. It turned out that a Polish countess, who lived in Cornwall Gardens, had been murdered on the up-line platform of the Piccadilly Line. She had managed to stagger to the lift, where she said, "Bandits! Bandits!" to the lift attendant before expiring. By a strange coincidence, I had been up to town and returned the previous evening on the Piccadilly Line, but I arrived a little earlier, at the down-platform, of course, and saw and heard nothing. I am not sure whether they ever caught the assassins, who may have been involved in émigré politics.

Furse House panto Author at the back in the large hat. Rick Pollock, at the centre, became Mrs Thatcher's Russian interpreter

Prof. Wigzell recounts in some detail how we students wrote and put on a pantomime with the Wrens (with whom otherwise we could not mix). Will Ryan and I wrote the script, the hero lead was played by Rick Pollock, and Peter Oppenheimer gave a *tour de force* at the piano. Some of us dressed up as Wrens and sang a scurrilous song, "We are from Queen's Gate, Good girls are we. We are so proud of Our virginitee…" It got worse after that! Prof. Wigzell names a long list of alumni from the Russian course who made their names later in writing, acting, academia, and broadcasting, and stresses the influence on society at large that came from "a body of highly intelligent people with a deep love of Russian culture and the language itself". All of them, she concludes, remember this as an extraordinary period in their lives. This is undoubtedly true: in another book, about National Service, the author Prof. Richard Vinen says the only men who looked back with pleasure on their two years were linguists and pilots.

At the end of the course (for me, in 1958) came the last formidable test: the Civil Service Commission Interpretership. 60% was the pass mark and

CHAPTER TWO: NATIONAL SERVICE

80% was the "first class" level. Like most of the candidates I was somewhere in the middle. The intensity of the teaching, and the learning, had paid off.

For most of my time in London I had been Acting Petty Officer; now I became a Midshipman. I still had time to serve, and their Lordships were not quite sure what to do with qualified interpreters. Some went to the Admiralty to translate documents; some helped with the production of naval dictionaries; some went to GCHQ, and one or two assisted with Fishery Protection. My friend David Talks went to the Admiralty to help plot the movement of Soviet ships.

Our course was sent for a few weeks to Chatham, to learn how to be naval officers — how to kiss swords, how to be a divisional officer at sea (and look after your charges in the mess), and how to behave at wardroom dinners. At my first one, sitting in our best uniforms, as a small Royal Marine band played tunes from the shows in one corner, we sat down to a feast. Next to my place was a bowl of what I thought was consommé soup. I was just about to put my soup spoon in it, when I was saved by a white-gloved waiter behind me. To my eternal gratitude, he leaned forward and whispered, "That's your fingerbowl, sir". It was the first one I had ever seen (I'm just a lad from Scunthorpe!).

We also had to learn about court martial procedures and the treatment of naval prisoners in the 'glasshouse'. Amazingly, when we attended a real one, we all knew the first prisoner. He was Michael Leapman, later to become a prize-winning journalist and writer. But Michael did not like being in the Navy and he had not liked learning Russian. He found marching and rifle drill irksome. So he had been demoted to the level of stoker, and was compelled to perform menial tasks around Chatham barracks. He was charged with hitting a Petty Officer with a broom. The Petty Officer had clearly made a mess, ordered Michael to clean it up, Michael had refused; the order was then given again in the presence of the Officer of the Watch; it was given a third time in the presence of the Captain. At which point Michael raised the broom and hit the P.O. with the broom. After the evidence had been given, and it was clear Michael had disobeyed an order contrary to Queen's Regulations, he was sentenced to several days in the glasshouse.

But it did not end there, as the following day our trainee officers' course were due to visit the glasshouse, and when we got there the only prisoner visible, behind bars, was Michael. Some of our number said we should not talk to him. Others shouted, "Hello, Michael!" to the surprise of the accompanying officer. His incarceration was no bar to a bright future!

Maresfield

I was one of those sent to do an interrogation course at Maresfield, the HQ of the Intelligence Corps. I suppose the idea was that, in a cold war situation, there would be some of us who could question Russian naval prisoners in their own language and prise information out of them. Much of the course was fairly practical; and mindful of the Official Secrets Act, even 55 years later, I was cautious in my description of the course in a contribution to *The Coder Special Archive* (by Tony Cash and Mike Gerrard):

It was about keeping prisoners separate, keeping good records for comparison, deciding in advance what you need to find out, and distinguishing between operational information and that for long-term analysis. Some of the permanent staff of the Intelligence Corps were Russian speakers, and dressed up in uniform when pretending to be prisoners. They also had Russian weapons, such as guns, in a field. I do not recall being instructed to use any form of violence on prisoners, although sleep deprivation, irregular meals, and use of light/dark were permissible. The main aim was working in a team and putting together the information, like a jigsaw, to make a clear picture. One heard quite lurid stories about some of the permanent interrogators. Once, I recall, we were given a short talk by a visiting Russian general in full uniform before returning to Moscow. Why he was there was not really explained. Many of us were taken in – I believe he was an instructor. They liked doing that sort of thing.

The lurid stories, all unverifiable, included: putting British soldiers being trained to resist interrogation (marine commandos, paratroopers, and front line troops) into metal barrels and rolling them down a hill; tying them to stakes in a field, throwing a bucket of cold water over them and leaving them for the night; and fooling prisoners about the actual interrogation. I remember hearing that US pilots after an exercise were brought down to a bar on an aircraft carrier, and were engaged in conversation by a friendly chap, a bank manager by profession, while waiting to be called in for questioning. When they finally asked, "Say, when is this interrogation going to start?" they were told, "It's over". A more alarming story was that of an RAF squadron leader, who sat at a desk with a large, fierce, hungry dog on a leash at his side. Having managed to frighten his prisoner, he released him for a time into the outer room, where a nurse proffered a cup of tea, soothed him and asked how he felt, what was it that had upset him, and so on. It turned out that she was the wife of the Squadron Leader, and was the real interrogator. I also heard that a naval friend of mine on the Reserve, during a NATO exercise, ordered a German general under interrogation to take his trousers down. The humiliation was successful. All these stories - and no doubt there are many more – I have no personal evidence for. I was never a member of HMS *Ferret* at Ashford. Wikipedia says they have now moved to RAF Chicksands at Bedford.

David Talks says in his memoir that during an exercise at Maresfield, as part of the 'softening up' process:

At one point (I am ashamed to say) we put our prisoners into horizontal lockers and ran up and down on the lockers.

He had the task in role play of interrogating, in Russian, his friend Frank Knowles. David writes:

He became so exasperated with the process that he upset the desk where we sat and ran out of the building (where in real circumstances he would have been shot by a sentry).

David says he had a good laugh with a car park attendant in Norwich, when he discovered that the man had been a tank commander in the Soviet army and had been trained to interrogate possible British prisoners-of-war!

So our two years of conscription came to an end. After a couple of years the whole system, which must have been fairly costly to the state, was wound up. Brian Hawkins says "the good burghers of Crail were devastated to hear of the end of JSSL. Our students had made over the four years a tremendous contribution to the life of the community and would be much missed. Crail became something of a ghost town for several years after our departure until they suddenly discovered tourism." He estimates that about 5000 students went through the JSSL at Bodmin and Crail. He thinks it fair to say that they had the cream of national servicemen. 65% were already graduates, and a further 30% were proceeding to university after National Service.

A somewhat different view was taken by I.W. Roberts, the official historian of the School of Slavonic and East European Studies (SSEES) at London University. He sees the School as playing its part in assisting the government in teaching a language training programme devised by the War

CHAPTER TWO: NATIONAL SERVICE

Office. "The general level of attainment on the courses was high, with almost ninety percent of national servicemen passing the CSC Interpretership exam 'with not less than sixty percent of total marks'." He concludes: "Although the school was glad to assist the government in this way, it was not altogether sorry when the Ministry of Defence (War Office) decided, with the ending of conscription, in 1960, to set up its own Russian language schools and thus allow the School to devote more time to its normal academic work."

RNR Russian refresher course, BRNC Dartmouth 1979. Top row: Ron Truman, Tony Holcombe, Nigel Hawkins Michael Carter, Mike Webb, PH. Front row: David Wanstall (instructor), Martin Weir, Alex Rutherford (instructor) Gareth Jones, Philip Royle, Robert Avery (instructor)

Before we all went our separate ways, we were required to join the RNVR, or RNR as it soon became, to do a refresher course, for about three years. We were now in the Navy's Special Branch. It was stressed that considerable public expense had been invested in our skills and it was important to keep them up to scratch. So every year for a fortnight in the summer we would go off, initially to RAF Tangmere, then to the Defence School of Languages (formerly the RAEC centre) at Beaconsfield, where the instructors tried to devise means of keeping our Russian up to scratch, and later to BRNC Dartmouth.

15

CHAPTER TWO: NATIONAL SERVICE

Winched up in helicopter training at BRNC Dartmouth, on Reserve

16

We also studied the Soviet navy, and familiarised ourselves with the latest ships, their radars and their weapons. The important thing was to know how to translate the technical terms. If you opted to continue on the Reserve, as several of my friends and I did, one could opt for an Intelligence course. I did one at Ashford, where the Intelligence Corps were then based. It was a joint service affair and quite taxing. I continued on the Reserve throughout the 60s and 70s, rising to Lt. Cdr RNR, and was awarded the Reserve Decoration for my loyalty (R.D.) with the Clasp added after 25 years.

Chapter 3: Frinton

In 1985, with the numbers dwindling, the MOD decided to close down the Naval Russian Language Reserve. Closure was effective from April 1st. Jeffrey Wickham wrote of himself in a biographical theatre programme note, "Discharged from Naval Intelligence on All Fools' Day". On the final reserve Russian course, a number of us gathered for a meal in a fine restaurant in Dartmouth, the Carved Angel, and decided to form a society to allow us to meet occasionally in the future. There were nine founders (of whom, at the time of writing, seven still survive). We devised a title, an acronym of Former Russian Interpreters Of the Navy = the FRINTON Society. David Talks devised the logo. I became the first secretary, Robert Avery was the first Chairman. The letterhead was later printed for me, and provided, by former Lt. Cdr RN Gerry Taylor, who later went on the run, in October 1995, with the funds of Whitworth town council, near Rochdale where he was town clerk. He has never been seen again. He took around £130,000. His car was found by the police at Hull docks. And he signed for a purchase aboard a ferry to Zeebrugge. Frinton's first and only known master criminal!

FRINTON Society letterhead

Later, Admiral of the Fleet Sir Julian Oswald became the first President, succeeded by Rear-Admiral Bruce Richardson. Both cast a friendly and enthusiastic eye on our affairs for many years. With a little research, we found many ex-Russianists, and the society membership grew and grew, to include attachés, diplomats, submarine commanders, professors, actors, and many academics of distinction. We have held an annual dinner, in recent years at the Naval Club in London – though it has also been in a nuclear submarine wardroom at Faslane, at Eton College, at Rugby School, and several other slightly exotic locations. In the summer, one of us hosts a reception in a garden, a hotel or a private house. Or even aboard a warship. Now and then we have organised outings to the West End (for 'Interpreters') to Stratford (for 'The Spanish Tragedy') and to the Festival Hall (for the Bach choir, in which one of our number, Michael Goodden, was singing in Russian). Two or three times a year a 'Signal' is sent out, with articles and reports from far-flung parts of Russia and elsewhere. The society, over thirty years on, is thriving.

Brenda and Tony Holcombe (left) and Donald Richards (right) look on as I wonder what to do with a large metal plaque 'liberated' from an RN ship, with which I was presented.

Chapter 4: Cambridge to Moscow

I went up to Cambridge in 1958, and became a student journalist on *Varsity*. To go to all the political meetings, I joined all three political parties. To my surprise, in 1959 the Conservative students in C.U.C.A. offered a trip to Russia organised through the NUS at a ridiculously low rate of £32 for a 16-day trip. I signed up. To Moscow with the Tories! The group was led by Lord (Nick) Bethell, who spoke Russian. In the group was the tall, affable figure of Tom Adams, the son of Sir Grantley Adams, who came from Barbados, of which he later became Prime Minister.

Tom Adams, former head of the BBC Caribbean Service, later Prime Minister of Barbados.

We took a train across the endless flat lands of Eastern Germany, after a quick tour of Berlin before the Wall had gone up. We were given a trip in a bus down the dreary façade of Stalin Allee. Then across Poland to Warsaw, where we spent a night. Then on to the Russian border and Brest Litovsk, where we changed trains to a different gauge. Then across the endless flat lands of Belorussia, till we got to Moscow. It was the time just

20

after the Cuban revolution, and in Russia, Fidel was a hero. But it was evident that ordinary Russians had not seen many brown or black faces, and Cubans were an object of curiosity. So was Tom. He did not like being ordered about in a group by the *Intourist* guide and tended to wander off on his own. The next day he found that his camera was missing from his room. The rooms were usually cleaned by two men, and they didn't look like cleaners. I accompanied Tom to an interview with the hotel manager and interpreted for him. To no avail. The management knew nothing about it. Tom must have mislaid his camera.

One day Tom, who was a barrister (and later, head of the BBC Caribbean service) asked if he could see a Russian court in action. *Intourist* was not helpful, so we wandered off to try and find a court, which we eventually did. We walked into an ongoing case and sat in the visitors' seats. This caused a great stir. The case was temporarily suspended while we were summoned to the Judge's room to explain ourselves. I told the judge that Tom, as a barrister from England, was merely interested in Russian court procedures, and he seemed to be satisfied. The case was a dispute (and there were many like it) between adjoining tenants in a multi-storey block of flats. When a ruling was finally given (by the judge and two assessors), the citizens involved came up to us to tell us how satisfied they were and how just Soviet justice was.

We saw all the tourist sites, including the Mausoleum, where at that time both Stalin and Lenin were lying embalmed in transparent cases, under illumination. We had jumped the very long queue in Red Square. No-one protested. I then behaved in a way that, in retrospect, was rather juvenile. For some reason I was at the time wearing a straw hat. As I went in, a guard shouted, "Shlyapa! Shlyapa!" meaning that I should take my hat off, as in a church. This I did. But when I got round a corner, I put it back on again. When we arrived in the area where the embalmed bodies were, there were further armed guards but they had their heads bowed, so I got away with it. I am proud to be one of the few western visitors who refused to take his hat off to Stalin! Incidentally I noticed nicotine stains on Stalin's fingers. The flesh of Lenin was going slightly waxy. A year or two later, in 1961, as a consequence of Nikita Khruschev's repeated denunciations of Stalin to closed sessions of the 20th and 22nd Party Congresses, Stalin's body was removed from the Mausoleum. It was placed in the Necropolis just outside the Kremlin wall, where several other former leading, but less substantial, Soviet politicians are also buried. A friend recalls reading that

CHAPTER FOUR: CAMBRIDGE TO MOSCOW

Khruschev ordered the grave to be covered over with 2 metres depth of concrete to ensure Stalin did not re-emerge!

The Lenin Mausoleum in Red Square

Curiously, one place we were not welcome was the British Embassy. A group of students, including our interpreter Sasha, and Peter Hancock, who was to be President of the Cambridge Union, attempted to pay a courtesy visit to the Embassy. But, says Peter, they hardly got through the door before the Sergeant-at-Arms descended on them and told them to leave in no uncertain terms. They protested that they were a group of British students visiting Russia, but to no avail. They were told, "That bloke there is not a British student, he's a bleedin' Russian, so get out!" Peter adds that in those days relations with the Russians were very different, especially at the trade level; his family firm in Wales had contracts with the Admiralty to convert two Russian ships – formerly British frigates – into whale capturing vessels. In the seventies they also built barges for the Russians.

Some trivialities that I recall are the interest shown by Russian women in the high heels of some of the female members of our group, and our utter failure in the 'House of Friendship' to produce a 'national dance' when asked, after performances by many other groups of foreign students. Eventually we settled on a Scottish reel, with an English Milord at the piano, but we had to recruit Russian girls to join in and we got hopelessly mixed up. The day was slightly saved by an old Etonian, Brian Christopher, who was a spare-time magician. He produced a pack of cards and with a few neat tricks he saved the day for us! In Leningrad we mixed in with a group of students from Oxford, one of whose number, another British peer, Lord Corvedale, had driven them all the way in a red double-decker bus. On the train to Leningrad I foolishly fell in with some hard-drinking young Russians who made me swig glasses of vodka all in one go: I had to spend the following day nursing a hangover. I learned later that in another compartment, my friend Tom had produced a pack of cards, invited some Russians to a game of poker, and cleaned them out. One of my other friends was baffled when he declared, "Seven card stud, deuces wild, ace in the hole!" Elsewhere on the train, I am reliably informed, one or two of our group, who had served during National Service in Army Intelligence, had some fun talking to a rather drunken Tank Major in the Soviet Army. We also did a bit of black marketeering, selling biros, plastic macs, Y-fronts and second-hand Penguin books to Russian students; they were eagerly snapped up. The official rate was ten roubles to the pound, but on the streets, one of our number recalls, you could often be offered forty. One oddity was spotting the Labour leaders, Hugh Gaitskell and Aneurin Bevan, who were there on a fact-finding visit, emerging from a hotel doorway in Leningrad; another in our group saw Guy Burgess lunching in the Hotel Metropole.

Called out in the Red Press

When I returned, I wrote about my first impressions of Russia in the Cambridge university newspaper *'Varsity'*. I thought the women looked dowdy, and shunned make-up, and I wrote how the men wore poor quality clothes and dirty shoes. They were used to austerity. Their social attitudes were puritanical; they looked with disapproval at the high heels and shorter skirts worn by some of the women students in our party, And they said, "Shame!" and, "Disgusting!" to a French girl who wore her hair long down her back. I remarked in my article on the lack of advertisements on the Underground, and on the general view by Russians that the West was 'decadent'. I pointed to the lack of freedom in a controlled press, the lack of choice at election time, and the primitive anti-religious propaganda then prevailing. I concluded that our ideas on freedom and justice were irreconcilable.

CHAPTER FOUR: CAMBRIDGE TO MOSCOW

This may all seem pretty trite nowadays, but a big surprise was to follow: someone, possibly a pro-Communist student at Cambridge, must have forwarded the article, (which would be read at the most by ten thousand students in Cambridge), to the Soviet Embassy. Thence it went to Moscow, and the offices of *Komsomolskaya Pravda,* and a Mr L. Kuznetsov took it upon himself in a long article, to heap derision on it. 'Pettifogging rubbish' was the least of his barbs. His headline was 'The Feeble Arguments of Mr Hill'. This was a pun on my name. And he goes on to mock my assertion that there was no democracy in the USSR. Well, perhaps my views were a little naïve and pompous, but his were laughable. And the readership of *Varsity* in the USSR at that time (and probably now) was zero.

CHAPTER FOUR: CAMBRIDGE TO MOSCOW

Graduating with BA (Classics and Moral Sciences) Cambridge 1961

Chapter 5: Diplomatic Ping pong

Some years later, in the mid-60s, I was working as a producer of current affairs programmes in Bush House, and I went to the party conferences to produce reports for the General Overseas Service. Once, when I was relaxing in a Blackpool bar after a long day, I got into conversation with a man who turned out to be a Rumanian diplomat. He seemed affable enough and invited me to lunch with him when we were back in London. I accepted, and over the meal he questioned me a lot about British politics, (I think he probably had to write weekly reports) and my replies were no more than you could read in The *Daily Telegraph*. He was also interested in who I knew in the BBC Rumanian service, which put me on my guard. The truth was I knew no-one there. But I reported the encounter to naval security, as I was bound to do as a reserve officer.

A week or two later, I was informed that they were interested in my meeting, and asked if I could go to the War Office and see Mr Brown (I cannot remember his real name, but it was probably an *alias* anyway). He was a bluff sort of fellow in civilian clothes, and did not say what he was, though I could guess. He asked me if I would invite my Rumanian friend back to lunch, and ask him about his family, where he came from and as much personal detail as I could get. I said I would, but I was nervous about doing it. I feared he might realise what was going on. We had the lunch, and he persisted about the Rumanian service personnel. I don't think I was suspected. I found out a fair amount of detail about him, but when I reported back to Mr Brown, I said that was the last time I would do that sort of thing. I felt very uncomfortable. But that is what spies do: they get other people to do their dirty work.

Chapter 6: Reserve Training

Being in the RNR meant I was away for a fortnight every year, usually in July, at either Dartmouth or Beaconsfield. The Navy paid me (Lieutenant's rate, later that of Lieutenant Commander) and the BBC continued to pay me, so it was very useful extra cash for the summer holidays. Fortunately for me the Deputy Director-General was Alan Protheroe, himself a former senior officer in the Welsh Guards, and he approved of reserve training; there were others in the BBC (Clifford Luton and Christopher Lee come to mind) who were also reservists. Some employers were not so generous. A few years later a Trotskyite rag, the *Socialist Worker*, ran an article naming a number of us as government stooges within the BBC. I had my suspicions about who leaked the information, but it was unpleasant knowing there were colleagues in the BBC trying to undermine our credibility. I do not ever recall being told by the government of the day what to write and what to broadcast.

Chapter 7: Falklands 1982

I had reason to be grateful to Alan Protheroe in the spring of 1982 after Argentina invaded the Falklands. I was pleased to be selected to do the live radio commentary on the tense debate in the House of Commons on a Saturday morning, from the glass-fronted box at the end of the Chamber. Tempers boiled over once or twice when a Tory backbencher, who had served in the Foreign Office, suggested the seeking of a diplomatic compromise. He was roundly accused of defeatism. Fortunately for him this exchange happened in the few minutes during which we were off the air for the one o'clock news.

A few days after this, I did a piece for the news and the 'Today' programme after the *Sheffield* had been struck by an Exocet missile, causing serious casualties. A member of the Commons Defence committee pointed out to me that they had published, a few months earlier, a document showing that because of cost-cutting, the length of the ship had been shortened, and because of the extra weight involved, it could not carry the Seawolf missile. Only two frigates in the Task Force, Type 22s, were equipped with Seawolf. Moreover there had been long delays, because of deciding between two radar systems, in bringing the Seawolf into operation. The Defence committee was to meet shortly, in secret, and this matter was on the agenda. The chairman himself discussed this in the lobby with me, and later publicly wondered where I had got my information from. Lobby rules (which govern the behaviour of political journalists at Westminster) forbade me from naming my source! Moreover I heard that, in view of the speculation, suspicion among MPs had fallen on a Tory knight who left the meeting early, although in fact he was not my source, and he was only leaving to go to a BBC studio, to be interviewed on the *World at One*. The Minister for Defence Procurement, Lord Trenchard, got very agitated, and attacked me in the Lords for inaccuracy and making wrong inferences, and wrote to the BBC's chairman as well. 'Dear George....', it began. In my defence, I pointed out that I was working from published government documents, and that I myself was a Lt Cdr RNR, so had some understanding of the issues.

Alan Protheroe backed me, for which I was very grateful; so did the BBC's correspondence department, which drafted the Chairman's reply to

28

Trenchard; and also supportive was an old friend of mine, Lord Cledwyn, (formerly the Labour minister Cledwyn Hughes, who became chairman of the Parliamentary Labour Party) who I went to see privately. At the time he was Leader of the Opposition in the House of Lords. He very kindly wrote to me afterwards saying he did not believe anyone was blaming me personally.

Perhaps the ultimate comment on this troublesome period (for me) and national tension (for politicians, the armed services and their loved ones) came in the annual report by Mark Jones, the captain of my cricket team, the Bushmen. 'It is a curious fact', he wrote, 'in our game against the Brickbats, that our no.1 in the batting order (Peter Hill) and our no.5 (Michael Cockerell) were both named and censured in the House of Commons the previous week. The Historian confirms that this has not happened in June for some little time'.

Chapter 8: With Devonshire in Leningrad

My regular Reserve training really paid off when in 1966 I was called on to visit Russia again. The request came out of the blue, from the Admiralty. HMS Devonshire, supported by a Fleet auxiliary ship, the Oleander, was to pay an official visit to Leningrad. Interpreters were needed. I wrote an article about the visit some time later in 2007, for my fellow interpreters in the Frinton Society.

What follows is a slightly edited version.

HMS Devonshire

Warning Note: My memories are a little hazy after such a lapse of time, so where a little colour has been added I confess, retired journalist that I am, that my account may not always strictly conform with the veracity of events. However, Andrew Thomson and Robert Avery have helped me get nearer the truth, and express it correctly.

Some forty-one years ago, when we were all very young, I received a phone call from the Admiralty. It was the summer of 1966, the sun shone brightly, the World Cup was ours, and Harold Wilson had won his best election yet. "Would you be prepared, Lieutenant Hill, to go to Leningrad, where Devonshire is to pay a goodwill visit?" It is

CHAPTER EIGHT: WITH DEVONSHIRE IN LENINGRAD

a mystery why their Lordships' eyes had fallen on me, though I understood why they had also fallen on Martin Weir, a fellow RNR interpreter of maturer years, who combined canny Aberdonian affability with a real linguistic skill. When we eventually assembled, we discovered we were to sail in the RFA Oleander, a large auxiliary oiler of up to 39,000 tons displacement, named after a poisonous shrub (it later was renamed Olmeda). Also aboard was a Royal Marines band. Flying his flag aboard Devonshire, a County Class destroyer of 6,200 tons displacement, was Admiral Sir John Byng Frewen, C-in-C Home Fleet, known to his subordinates as "Black Jack". Fortunately he had a proper interpreter with him for serious meetings and speeches, in the person of Andrew Thomson, a full-bearded regular who had been Naval Attaché in Moscow.

Devonshire was a handsome ship, in the same class as Kent, Hampshire and London, armed with Seaslug and Sea Cat surface-to-air missiles. I learned all about its power plant, range, and armament from the Leningradskaya Pravda when we arrived. These details were not given in the official handout.

My first strong memory is of being on the bridge of Oleander about a day after sailing in early September. It was early morning, just off Kiel, and very foggy. The officers on watch were following the radar track of Devonshire, slightly ahead of us, and were fascinated to see it coalesce with another large bright dot on the screen. It emerged that the pride of the Royal Navy had just collided with a stationary tanker. The bow of a moored tanker had torn away all the handrails on the port side of the upper deck, denting the Avgas tanks without causing them to ignite or explode, and there was a fair amount of mangled metal. The Admiral was not amused – especially as the boat davits holding his splendid barge had been split, so the barge had to be transferred by crane to Oleander. I saw all this as we pulled alongside in the Kiel Canal. Being on a much larger ship, we had a grandstand view. I believe there was an enquiry and court martial sometime later, but the immediate problem was to get it all covered up with tarpaulin before proceeding. In the wardroom of Oleander there was quiet amusement among the Merchant Navy seadogs at the predicament of RN.

The strategy, apparently, was that we should tell all Russian visitors to the ship that under the tarpaulins was secret equipment we were not allowed to show. With most Russians this was immediately accepted. So on we sailed through the Baltic. Devonshire was moored to head and stern buoys off the embankment in the centre of Leningrad, to be visible to all for this five-day visit. Was it starboard side to the quay? I think so - it would have been sensible! The more workmanlike Oleander was moored to buoys a mile or so off Kronstadt – far enough off for the range of most binoculars. We were given a Russian liaison officer called Mike, who only wanted to drink Coca Cola and watch western videos; the real power was his signals rating, who stayed on the bridge wing, scowling when he wasn't signalling.

CHAPTER EIGHT: WITH DEVONSHIRE IN LENINGRAD

The general idea, as stated by the Admiral, was that the people of Leningrad were free to come aboard Devonshire and look round. The ship's ratings were smartly dressed and placed at key locations to help. However, it soon became clear that access to the ship was being controlled by a sort of guardhouse on the quay, and they only allowed visitors who had tickets through it to the boat ferrying. These had clearly been carefully distributed to party members, trade unionists, shop stewards, troublemakers, spies etc. I tried to get a couple of friendly youths who lacked tickets through the control in my company, but failed. Also admitted to the ship were nasty little groups of Komsomoltsi wearing red armbands, who went around the deck harassing the other Russians. I recall one old man coming up to me and saying "Do you have a doctor aboard? I'm a doctor and I would like to speak to him." I went below to find the ship's doctor. When I returned the old fellow was being hustled towards the gangway by the teenage thought police, and that was that. I recall being extremely peeved.

One of my allotted duties for some reason was to collect all the postcards written by the ratings and post them. My experience with the old doctor had turned me paranoid, and I decided not to post them in the post box conveniently placed next to the guard house: I spent several hours one afternoon walking round Leningrad city posting six cards in one box, six in another....there's no way the KGB were going to discover the home addresses of the crew's loved ones without a major intelligence operation at the sorting office!

Another of my duties was to escort ashore a selection of the crew of Oleander for a visit to Peter the Great's summer palace. Two elderly ladies spouted facts like the fountains they were describing, and the torrent of statistics about hectares and cubic litres of water was too much for the somewhat subversive lads I was interpreting for. Discipline with them was a loose concept. Every time I turned round there seemed to be rather fewer than we set out with, until only a rather serious-minded chippie with good manners remained. I had earlier given the group a short lecture on behaviour when ashore: do not get drunk, do not get into fights, do not try to pick up women (there are no prostitutes in Leningrad, ha! ha!) and do not take English currency ashore and exchange it for roubles. When it came to departure time on the fifth day, there emerged onto the quay from the side streets all the lads in the Oleander crew, with their arms wrapped round the ladies of Leningrad; one later told me they had taken their money ashore, paid for women and parties, and spent most of the time drinking. Still, nobody as far as I know was arrested!

Andrew Thomson, unbeknown to me, had given a similar lecture over the internal TV to Devonshire's crew. The KGB could well try to trap or blackmail them. They might try to buy items of clothing from them and film the exchange. "Don't sell your socks," he concluded. Sure enough a sailor returned under the influence, minus his socks. But his advice was ignored at a somewhat higher level. He had warned officers to go ashore together in case of attempted kidnap. He himself took some officers ashore to see the

CHAPTER EIGHT: WITH DEVONSHIRE IN LENINGRAD

sights, and at one point was overtaken by a very fast walker, who hissed, "Buy your socks?" as he shot past. It was Black Jack Frewen, out for a constitutional, alone!

Andrew Thomson also recalls an unpleasant encounter with a GRU man who accompanied some Russian officers to a Sunday evening buffet and film in Devonshire's Wardroom. He was "a narrow-eyed cold fish called Byeloglazkin – not a gentleman." A Russian officer told Andrew he was KGB. It turned out that the film, chosen by the Commander, Ken Mills, was Born Free – an innocent story about animals with no possible political nuances – but with a title open to misinterpretation. After supper Byeloglazkin snapped his fingers and ordered all the Russian officers to leave. Andrew translated the subsequent discussion, during which Mills made it very clear he was not prepared to put up with such a display of bad manners. Andrew concludes "The GRU weasel thought briefly and ushered his flock back into the Wardroom to watch lions."

One of the big events was an on-board dinner given by the Admiral in the wardroom for senior officers of the Baltic Fleet. When I went to inspect the place settings, I noticed that there were two different kinds of silver place-card holders. Most of the British officers had a silver dolphin leaping upwards. Most of the Russians had a Chinese labourer, at those times known as a coolie, bearing the card on its back. Coincidence? The dinner for me was fairly tedious as the English captain to my left, whom I was supposed to interpret for, insisted on practising his execrable Russian straight across me. But things warmed up towards the end when Sir John, who had served in wartime escorts on convoys to Russia, as well as having commanded the aircraft carrier Eagle, made a speech reminding the Russians of the enormous amount of equipment and planes that had been brought round to Murmansk in the last war at great cost. None of this appeared in the Russian press. He then sent a steward out, who brought in an engraving of his distant ancestor, Admiral John Byng, being shot on the quarterdeck of HMS Monarch in March 1757 for his failure to take Minorca. "I always carry this at sea with me", he said with a wry smile, "to remind me that Admirals are not indispensable". A bullet-headed colonel of the Leningrad Garrison leaned forward and said to me in Russian, "It is not unknown in our country!"

Martin Weir recalls a welcoming banquet ashore to repay the Admiral's hospitality: he found himself interpreting for the Director of the Hermitage Museum. Andrew Thomson interpreted for the Admiral at several events, notably the dinner ashore given by Rear Admiral Ivan Ivanovich Baikov, the Leningrad Naval Commander. He recalls: 'Eventually Baikov noted that Frewen was drinking only water. "Why does the Admiral not drink?", he asked. "Tell him, Thomson", replied Sir John, "that I do not drink." Baikov: "In Soviet Union, we shoot Admirals who do not drink." Sir John: "Tell him, Thomson, that I have a stomach ulcer". "Ah, so do I!" said Baikov, and he downed another vodka.'

CHAPTER EIGHT: WITH DEVONSHIRE IN LENINGRAD

For those who had to return to Oleander out in the bay, a Russian motorboat was provided. However, there are several timber yards at the mouth of the Neva and on this occasion the motorboat, I assume, hit a submerged log, because the engine suddenly cut out and we started wallowing quite badly without power. Embarrassment all round. This was somewhat relieved, for the Russians at least, by watching one of the interpreters throwing up on the cabin floor. And it wasn't Martin Weir!

During the five-day stay there were many events – wreath-laying, dinners, sporting contests – the local press told me our boys were beaten 9-1 at water polo – but the ceremony I remember best was Beating Retreat by the Royal Marines band on the deck of Devonshire. It had started badly for me. The previous year, at the request of the GB-USSR Association, I had entertained a visiting Russian academic to an evening out in London. He was a fairly agreeable Professor of Cybernetics at Leningrad University. I had been in civvies, accompanied by Chris Dowman, and had not mentioned the Navy. Just my luck, as I stood in my best uniform greeting guests at the top of the gangway, to see the self-same chap coming aboard with his wife. He gave me a frosty look. Through clenched teeth he murmured "I think we have met before!" And that was the last word he said to me. However, his wife was more friendly, and as the white ensign came down, and Sunset was sounded by a lone bugler in counterpoint to "Abide with Me", tears were falling down her cheeks. "Please do not lose your traditions," she confided.

Leaving Leningrad for Helsinki was perhaps the most traumatic event for Martin and me. It took place at night. The idea was to prevent Devonshire's officers viewing the work in progress in shipyards along the Neva. Aboard Oleander a Russian pilot was provided on the bridge, which was a long way away from the quarterdeck, where Martin and I were posted to transmit orders to the Russian crew of a small tug, who were supposed to slip the mooring lines from buoys. Martin and I crouched under a housing, with our Russian dictionaries and torches at the ready, hoping against hope that we would understand what came next. "Slip the after messenger!" was the order, I recall. We knew that. Robert Avery can be proud. The tug then lowered a couple of crew into the water to unhook the ship's mooring line from a barrel buoy. Unfortunately they couldn't undo it. They were getting cold and things were getting tense. The ship was beginning to swing around. Eventually deck crew on Oleander were ordered to sever the cable on the deck – with axes, I seem to recall. This took a short time and made a lot of sparks. The severed cable rushed through the hawser over the side and hit the water with a great splash. The weight of it spun the barrel buoy, and threw the poor men on it into the air. Oleander was putting out to sea. Our interpreters' mission was accomplished.

Chapter 9: Weekend Exercise

I cannot recall the precise date, but while I was working at Westminster as a journalist, I was approached by the press office of the Ministry of Defence and asked if I would help them out with an exercise they were planning for a forthcoming weekend. I said yes, and kept it very quiet. It turned out to be a very prudent and realistic exercise in how senior civil servants, senior military officers and perhaps senior politicians and ministers, would react to a nuclear accident on British soil. I will not go into the details, even today. I am sure such exercises continue even now in a more modern guise. And I am glad they do. My role was to write pretend newspaper articles, headlines, and editorials, in response to the information that was coming out from Ministry of Defence sources about the very serious accident. These would be fed back to the decision makers to give them an idea of media reaction (this was in the days before social media). As I was tucked away in a small room by myself, I was not aware of how many other people were involved, or at what level, although I did talk to a senior Captain RN in the medical branch, who was an expert in nuclear medicine. I tried to do a good job and felt that, though tiring, it was a small but worthwhile contribution. I told none of my work colleagues.

Chapter 10: Helping an Architect

A much less confidential, and even pleasurable task came my way, when I was approached by the well-known architect Donald Insall, who lived not far from me on Kew Green. He was awarded the CBE, and in 2010 knighted for his outstanding work on conserving historic buildings. The list of his projects is impressive. He was being visited by two leading Russian professors who were interested in British historic buildings, and in seeing how the National Trust worked. I cannot remember why I was asked, but it was an agreeable task to escort them to a number of sites and either explain, or interpret, for officials they met. One evening we were invited to dinner at Donald Insall's house and I interpreted for the dinner party. My wife was impressed by the wide reading of the visiting professors, particularly of English classics like Dickens and Jack London.

Sir Donald Insall

CHAPTER TEN: HELPING AN ARCHITECT

Pastel portrait of the author by Elizabeth Passini, 1974

Chapter 11: Ian Trethowan

Sir Ian Trethowan, Director-General of the BBC

In late 1979, out of nowhere, came an exciting opportunity. It started with me going into the office at the Commons one day and the secretary said: "You are asked to report to the D.G.'s office at 2pm". Good Lord, what had I done? Had I said something on the air which had caused a protest at the top level and the Director-General was going to tick me off, or fire me? I was not given a clue, so I made my way to Broadcasting House and the office of Ian Trethowan, whom I happened to know a little because he had been to the same school as me (Christ's Hospital), whence he had left early for a humble job in Fleet Street, and risen to be a senior lobby correspondent and, because he was very good on TV, to be co-presenter of the weekly TV programme "Gallery" and "The Week in Westminster" with Peter Hardiman Scott. He was often in our Commons office, sitting in the only armchair, and sometimes locked away in the phone booth-cum-studio at the far end, where he was suspected of talking to his bookmaker. He became head of BBC radio and in 1977, D.G. (As an aside, I was once sitting at my desk in the office reading the weekly notes of the meeting held by the BBC's Editor of News and Current Affairs, and I read that it had been decided to have a quiet word with Mr Trethowan for expressing too overtly Conservative views in his column in the *Times*. At that very moment, Ian was sitting about three feet away from me! Thank goodness I had the good sense not to say, "Hey, Ian, have you seen this?")

So there I was, being shown into the D.G.'s office for reasons unknown. He was extremely friendly. "Take a seat, Peter. Would you like a coffee?" So it wasn't going to be all bad.

"Well", he said, "I understand you speak Russian. I have to go to Moscow to sign some agreements about the exchange of TV programmes, and the visit of a Russian circus. I am going with my wife and another BBC couple, and we will be doing quite a bit of sightseeing and dining out – so would you like to come with us as interpreter?" He was keen to have someone of his own who could negotiate in shops and restaurants, and make sure the Russian official interpreters were doing their job properly. Who could say 'No' to that? I was still doing my Russian Reserve training with the Navy every year, so I was reasonably up to scratch. I rang some of my teachers and mentors at the Defence School of Languages, and we got together word lists that might be useful in TV and radio studios. I watched Russian videos. I read Russian newspapers. I really got myself up to speed. And then….

In December 1979 the Soviet Union invaded Afghanistan. There was international outrage, particularly on the part of the new British Prime Minister, Mrs Thatcher. It was decided by those at the top of the BBC that it would be unwise at such a time for the BBC to be visiting Moscow for friendly exchanges with the Russian broadcasters, so the visit was called off. So all my homework went to waste. And the visit was never revived.

Chapter 12: Moscow and Georgia

British journalists meeting the bosses of the Supreme Soviet inside the Kremlin, December 1987

Late in 1987 I was invited by John Roberts of the GB-USSR Association to join a group of journalists on a visit to the Soviet Union. We were to be the guests of the Soviet Union of Journalists. It was a return visit after some Russian journalists had come to Britain, and I had taken part in the talks. Among the group going out were some top Fleet Street men: Hugo Young (*Guardian*), Neal Ascherson, (*Observer*), John Miller (*Daily Telegraph*) and Geoffrey Smith (*Times*). We had some fairly unproductive meetings round a large table with Soviet journalists, who were unwilling to concede much in the presence of their colleagues. We met the editor of *Izvestia* which was more promising. He asked us, "What is the difference between a Minister and a fly? Answer: none. Both can be killed by a newspaper!" We met a sociologist who was trying to devise honest public opinion polls in a hostile climate. And we did the usual round of tourist sites. However, for a change of scene, our hosts decided to take us to Tbilisi in Georgia for a day or two to show us one of the USSR's southern Republics, Georgia. Our official Russian interpreter rather despised the 'Stans', suggesting to us they were corrupt and run by extended ruling families.

CHAPTER TWELVE: MOSCOW AND GEORGIA

The outstanding Georgian at the time was Eduard Shevardnadze, Foreign Minister of the USSR and later to be President of Georgia. He stood alongside Gorbachev in promoting *perestroika*.

We found Georgia, or at least, Tbilisi, rather charming, with its gardens festooned with vines in a warm climate (very unlike Moscow) and with houses in a distinctive local architectural style. We had little time for visits except to a puppet theatre and to a museum, where there was a room showing the achievements of Soviet cosmonauts. I noticed in a large photograph that one of them had the word MONGOLIA written across the top of his helmet. I turned aside to one of my journalist friends and remarked, "Good God, the Mongols got to the moon before we did!" Unfortunately, an English speaking Russian curator heard me – and burst into loud laughter!

Twenty years on from our visit, in 2008, I wrote a piece (in the historic present tense) for Radio 4's programme, *'From Our Own Correspondent'* about how the adventure turned out very differently from the way the Russians intended:

A Visit to Georgia

We are in Tbilisi Airport, in Georgia, in the Soviet Union's Deep South. We've been waiting all day for a plane to take us back to Moscow. No announcements are made. We sit, hungry and frustrated, reading pamphlets by Boris Yeltsin, the disgraced Moscow party boss, which the Georgians have conveniently forgotten to remove from the racks. A detachment of Algerian soldiers arrives, speaking Arabic. At last, after eight hours, our flight is announced. We've missed three important meetings with officials in Moscow, but we feel relief – two hours and we'll be there. We board the plane and strap ourselves in, amid a crowd of Russians and Georgians.

Suddenly there's an announcement by the stewardess: "We will be making an unscheduled stop at Grozny." Grozny? There's a murmur all down the plane. Where's that? Why are we stopping? A stewardess appears and is eagerly questioned. "We haven't got enough kerosene to get us to Moscow," she says unapologetically, and moves on.

So we take off, and after nearly an hour we put down at Grozny, which we have discovered during the flight is the capital of the Chechen-Inguish Autonomous Republic in the Northern Caucasus. Rumour has it that you only have to drill a hole in the

CHAPTER TWELVE: MOSCOW AND GEORGIA

ground there, and oil spurts out.

So our Tupolev-154 lands with brakes screeching on a bumpy runway. "Please remain seated," says the stewardess. Then the pilots and cabin crew emerge, and try to walk down the gangway in their splendid blue and gold uniforms. But they don't get far. "Why didn't you warn us?" shouts the lady in front of me. "I'm going to miss my connections in Moscow now," says the lady beside me. "Why isn't there enough petrol kept in Tbilisi?" asks a third. The language gets stronger and bluer. "Don't you swear at me," says the chief pilot, his voice rising. "It's not my responsibility. I only fly the plane".

And as the shouts increase, and the mood turns ugly, the pilot strides past with his crew, and disembarks. "What about perestroika?" a woman shouts after them with heavy irony. We are soon told to follow, while refuelling takes place. As we stand around on the tarmac in the dark, we see hundreds of people walking the other way, to other aircraft. Shouted exchanges in the gloom reveal that previous flights have also been putting down at Grozny for fuel, no-one knows for how long. After 45 minutes in the Grozny air terminal, pausing only to read the latest news from the Washington summit in the Saturday edition of the Grozny Worker, we take off and get to Moscow at half past ten, twelve hours after we left our hotel in Tbilisi. It is twenty degrees below zero, and the man who's supposed to meet us with a bus has cleared off.

This whole, wonderfully Russian, experience rather spoilt the considerable efforts by our Georgian hosts to create a good impression. Because there's no doubt that Georgia, although part of the Soviet Union, is certainly nothing like Russia. It has its own language, its own culture, its own proud history; its climate is sub-tropical, and palm trees grow in the streets; tea bushes grow in the hills, vines grow in every backyard, and there are ski resorts in the high Caucasus.

Tbilisi is a city of galleried houses and old city walls, with lovingly preserved bathhouses and a multitude of cafés to sit out in. Alright, you can't order a vodka nowadays – it's more likely to be mint-flavoured mineral water – but the food is distinctly Georgian. They're specially proud of their local bread, and there's an atmosphere of natural abundance – you never see long queues for citrus fruits here as you would in Moscow – because Georgia is where they come from.

There's a greater air of political and religious tolerance too in Georgia. Make no mistake, it's a Communist republic with a central committee, a KGB, and all the usual apparatus of Soviet communism. But it seems less intrusive, and only 6% of the population of just over five million are Russian. There's a mix of Armenians, Azerbaijanis and Greeks, as well as Georgians, and they're proud that Jews have lived among them too – though they're puzzled that many Jews now want to leave. Christianity came in the third century AD, and though many monasteries and orthodox churches have now been turned into monuments, museums and theatres, about 5% of the people still attend church, and ecclesiastical architecture is restored.

One of their greatest treasures is the large collection of historic icons removed to Paris before the revolution, now returned to Tbilisi Art Museum; Mrs Thatcher signed the visitors' book there in April, expressing warm admiration. The irony is that the building where they are displayed is the seminary where Joseph Stalin studied for the priesthood for five years before being chucked out. And there's another small paradox: Stalin is still a hero in Georgia. "He won the war, didn't he?" was one comment I heard, and his birthplace (at Gori) is open to visitors. Whereas in Moscow, the press is showing signs of opening up once more the terrible history of the Thirties, when Stalin had a whole generation of leaders imprisoned or liquidated. Russians aren't too popular in Georgia – there were protest marches a few years ago when they tried to drop from Georgia's constitution the clause guaranteeing the use of the Georgian language in schools. Edward Shevardnadze, then Georgia's party boss, had to come out to the crowd and promise to have it put right. And when we saw a charming Georgian play in a puppet theatre, the one unmistakeable figure of fun was the Russian secret agent in his fur cap and overcoat. As far as one can tell, there's no overt Georgian nationalist or separatist movement. But whether they've got enough petrol or not, the Georgians are not going to let the Russians interfere with their own distinctive heritage.

A trip on the metro

Perhaps my view in August 2008 was short-sighted: South Ossetia broke away from Georgia in 1991, shortly followed by Abkhazia; Russians and Georgians fought, with some atrocities and ethnic cleansing, until a ceasefire was agreed in May 1994; the two mini-states are recognised by only five countries at the UN (including Russia).

While I was in Moscow on this trip, I performed a small service which had some scary moments. A college friend of mine, Alan Howard, asked me, if I was going to Moscow, I would take some books to a Jewish maths teacher, who had been subjected to harassment and persecution, on behalf of an organisation dedicated to helping Jewish prisoners of conscience. I agreed. One afternoon at the weekend in Moscow when nothing much was happening, I took the Moscow Metro to the station near where this man lived. However on the way I became aware of a young man in jeans who seemed to be following me, and was over-attentive to my movements. Whether this was paranoia, I don't know; whether he was plain-clothes

CHAPTER TWELVE: MOSCOW AND GEORGIA

KGB or whether he was just interested in my Western clothes and looking to buy or sell something I don't know. At any rate, I did not want to give away the man I was going to visit, whom I had telephoned in advance, so I got out at an earlier station and came back to the centre of Moscow. I rang my contact again the following day and decided to have another go at reaching him. This time I succeeded. He was a very nice man and very pleased to receive the books. He was at the time forced to work in an elementary school teaching arithmetic. He told me he was hoping to get an exit visa to Israel. He said it was very fortunate that I had turned round the previous day, as there had been a protest demonstration organised in central Moscow, and the KGB had posted a car outside his block of flats, presumably either to stop him joining the protest, or to observe whether he went. Had I arrived with my present in the sight of the KGB, I might have been in trouble, and even got myself arrested. It was with great pleasure a year or two later that I met him in London: he was now a Professor of Mathematics in the Technion, the leading Israeli university, in Haifa.

This escapade made me rather nervous and I spoke to the journalist group's leader, John Roberts, and told him what I had done, in case there were any repercussions: but there were none.

Chapter 13: Gerald Carroll

Gerald Carroll

I was to return to Russia a few more times in my life, and to meet with Russians in the Far East; but first came a bizarre few months working for a very strange man. I had left the BBC staff in the spring of 1992, so was looking for freelance jobs. Somehow, and I cannot remember how, I came into the employ of Gerald Carroll, a so-called millionaire property developer with plush offices in Queen Anne's Gate near Westminster. He was head of the Carroll Foundation, which included a large number of companies. Among the directors of these companies, who included several big names, was Sir Curtis Keeble, a very shrewd and likeable former British Ambassador to the USSR. I got on well with him. I also met around the office a man who was also the Conservative party organiser, Sir Anthony

CHAPTER THIRTEEN: GERALD CARROLL

Garner. Gerald wanted a Russian-speaking assistant. He was often in contact with the Russian embassy and he had his finger in a number of Russian pies. He had plans to build an office block, with a hotel and trade centre, over a Metro station entrance in Moscow. He had plans to bring Western agricultural machinery to the sugar beet fields and villages of Southern Russia. His companies also built a shopping mall over the A1(M) Motorway at Hatfield, but it went way over budget.

Gerald had a fine house in Newmarket where he also had a stud farm, and he sponsored races at Newmarket racecourse. He also had a collection of classic cars. His money had come from the family building firm built up by his father in Essex. He had a Range Rover with a registration plate A1, or something very like it, in which I occasionally travelled with him. And he seemed to own the private side of Farnborough airport, where he entertained lavishly during the Farnborough air show. When he was there, during the show, I was sent off to bring over the Russian test pilots to his marquee and viewing platform - they had arrived with a very large heavy-lift MIL helicopter, manufactured in Rostov-on-Don. My job, having fetched them, was to interpret for them and entertain them at Gerald's table. He had the idea of getting an airworthiness certificate in Britain for MIL helicopters, and marketing them. Despite advice to the contrary, he persisted in this. I would go to Westminster Public Library every Friday and read all the aircraft and commercial flying magazines I could find (without his permission) and photocopy relevant articles for him. Sometimes he was very pleased, without asking why I was doing this. I tried, as did others, to get him to see reality. On another occasion I accompanied him to the Naval and Military Club (I am not sure whether he was ever in the Army or the Navy) for a dinner with a senior Russian aircraft designer.

One day he asked me to find a British paint manufacturer who would be willing to paint the air terminal buildings at Rostov-on-Don. I managed to persuade one or two senior sales representatives that this was a worthy cause. But when I said to Gerald, "Who is going to pay for it?" He replied, "They will just have to punt for it." This apparently meant that *they* paid. I felt very sorry for the man from Crown who had come all the way to Gerald's office only to discover this troublesome fact. He was not much pleased. Gerald tried to suggest that there would be further contracts in Russia in the offing if the paint company took the bait, but it did not work. Meanwhile the MIL helicopter crew languished for weeks on end, unpaid,

CHAPTER THIRTEEN: GERALD CARROLL

in a Farnborough hotel, waiting for everything to get sorted out.

I eventually said to Gerald that, with my qualifications and linguistic skills, I was not prepared to work for him for ten pounds an hour. I said to him that it was then the going rate for gardeners. He replied that I was 'mercenary' and that the rate would go up when the 'Agro-industrial' deal was finalised. I saw no prospect of this, and walked out.

Perhaps my greatest achievement during this surreal period was finding out all about sugar beet machinery in Russia (mostly British made), and about the technical words in Russian for all the agricultural chemicals and fertilisers, manufactured by a division of ICI, which could be applied to sugar beet, to improve the Russian crop yields. But this was another of Gerald's schemes which came to nought.

In the early nineties Gerald Carroll went bankrupt, owing many millions. He claimed there had been fraud. His trusts, foundations, projects, and dreams all collapsed. He was a thin, square-shouldered, direct man, whose speech could be sharp. I was glad to be out before the roof fell in.

Chapter 14: Christopher Stephenson

Author with Christopher Stephenson at the door of the Ministry of Foreign Affairs in Moscow

Not long after this I fell in with Christopher Stephenson (perhaps through the good offices of Curtis Keeble) who was looking for an interpreter to accompany him to Moscow. He was an up-market estate agent (I believe

CHAPTER FOURTEEN: CHRISTOPHER STEPHENSON

he had previously worked buying and selling stud farms and racing stables) who was well-known in the Lambourn valley. He had previously been an army officer, and then trained to become an FRICS (a Fellow of the Royal Institution of Chartered Surveyors). He was a fairly short man, who had been an amateur jockey in his time, and a racehorse owner. His friends regarded him as an amusing *bon viveur*. I was never quite sure who he was working for, although cheques for payment for my services came from Orb Estates, which later went into liquidation and was wound up. Christopher had managed through a friend to sell a Russian property in Kensington Palace Gardens to the brother of the Sultan of Brunei, and he found favour in Moscow. He went there with Lord Milford Haven and signed an agreement with the Russians to help dispose of a number of redundant buildings around the world. So the aim was clear: the USSR had collapsed, and the Russian Federation wanted to find new owners for their properties. One, which I visited, was in Danang, in North Vietnam; one was in Hanoi; another was in Santiago in Chile.

Working for Christopher was both easy, and hard; it was difficult to get him to agree to a fee before we set off, and I usually presented him with a rough contract before we departed and got him to sign it. And the cheques took a long time to arrive. But he liked living in style: we stayed at the Metropole in the heart of Moscow, and dined in its best restaurants. We went by car to the Ministry of Foreign Affairs, one of the Stalin-era 'wedding-cake' skyscrapers, where we were escorted to the rooms of a Deputy Foreign Minister, an important and experienced man, who was much concerned at the time with mediating over the situation in Abkhasia (which as we have seen, subsequently broke away from Georgia). He had a very personable Russian interpreter, with whom I formed a friendship (which continued when he was posted with his wife and child to London). Fortunately *he* did most of the hard work. There were subsequent follow-up talks with architects, engineers and so on about the potential for converting redundant properties. It all seemed to go well, though I was never aware of a deal being sealed. I was annoyed with Christopher one evening when we were having a drink at the Metropole bar; to my surprise there were a few hookers in short skirts around the place, with their grim leather-clad minders sitting in the corner. I had thought this was a good class hotel. For a joke, Christopher said to one of them, as he went off to the loo, "Look after my father for me!" I didn't laugh.

CHAPTER FOURTEEN: CHRISTOPHER STEPHENSON

Mugged in Moscow

A much more serious event occurred when I tried to take the Metro to visit the BBC Office in Moscow. As I stood on the platform at Teatralnaya station, I was surrounded by about half a dozen teenagers, who included some girls, and they grabbed me. In what was obviously a well-planned manoeuvre, two of them pinned my arms behind me and two more went into my side pockets. Fortunately, I was wearing a heavy overcoat, buttoned and belted. I shouted out loudly in Russian, "HELP! Help me!" but nobody stirred, and there were a good many Russians waiting near me. They had clearly seen it all before. Within a few seconds a train arrived. I wrestled free and jumped onto it. Mercifully they did not follow me. Someone said to me later there were gangs doing this on a regular basis to foreigners, or those who looked foreign. I felt very stressed, and took some time to calm down. All the gang got from me was the key card to my hotel room. I went straight back and told the desk. They were easily able to cancel my card and issue a new one. The key cards do not bear a room number on them. This was the only time in my life when I have been physically assaulted.

Working for Christopher was not plain sailing. We got on fairly well and I was managing the official interpretation quite well: that was what he was paying me for. However, he often invited officials to dinner, and expected me to entertain them, in Russian, till a late hour; he did not see this as work. And the later the hour, the more the drink, and the filthier the stories. I said to Christopher I wanted extra pay for this sort of thing, which in some ways was linguistically harder for me, a non-professional. And when we had to wait over a weekend for a meeting with a minister on a Monday, he did not think I should be paid for the extra three days I was on call. I am afraid that I did.

So, on subsequent visits I asked him to sign a more carefully worded invoice, at a higher daily rate, to include both formal and informal sessions. I am glad to say he agreed. I am sure other interpreters have run into similar problems with their principal.

A month or two later he wanted me to go to Santiago with him. But the invitation came out of the blue and I was busy. He asked me to find another interpreter for him, which I did. He was an Oxford don, and far better than me with the language.

CHAPTER FOURTEEN: CHRISTOPHER STEPHENSON

Hong Kong and Hanoi

The most exciting trip of all was to Hanoi. Few westerners had been there. But the Russians had a seven-acre plot in down-town Hanoi, which could have been turned into a profitable housing estate – there were half-built houses with services there already. And they had a consulate in Danang, which was surplus to requirements. Christopher thought it best to fly direct to Hong Kong first and get over jet lag, before proceeding to Hanoi: so we had a couple of nights in the air-conditioned Metropole Hotel to recover. And we stayed there on the way back as well.

The Metropole Hotel in Hanoi

I did a few watercolours from the very top of the hill overlooking Hong Kong; and I witnessed the unexpected sight of the city's parks full of Filipino maids enjoying their Sunday off together. I marvelled at the old fashioned trams, and took a boat out to a fishing village to get a bit more atmosphere. But the weather was getting up and a typhoon was on the way: all doors and windows had to be locked shut and the hotel issued firm instructions to all its guests. When it died down we took a plane, a rather older Soviet-style airliner, to Hanoi. I remember coming in low over the paddy fields and watching the buffaloes working there.

Hanoi was a French city, again to my surprise, with a picturesque lake, wide boulevards and Victorian architecture; but there was little motorised traffic. Instead bicycles and scooters were everywhere, often with their riders balancing goods on either side. In the warmth of the evening, Vietnamese people sat out on the pavements eating. Some friends, who knew a mutual friend, came round to our hotel to take me out for a drink: and it was for a Guinness in O'Flaherty's Irish bar! (I forget the real name, but it was similar). When I came out of my room on the second floor, I heard the unmistakable voice of Douglas Hurd. He was the British Foreign Secretary in John Major's government and was paying the first ever such visit to North Vietnam since the war ended. His voice echoed up the stairwell as he briefed journalists travelling with him. I went down and there at the back was an old cricketing colleague, Chris Greene, who was at the time head of the BBC Vietnamese Service. I went up behind him and murmured, "Dr Livingstone, I presume?"

Christopher got down to negotiations, with the help of a few well-placed bottles of duty-free whisky, and we inspected the site, and talked to Vietnamese and Russians about it. He sent me to a venue where I was to meet the key Russian diplomat, but I could not see him. There was a Chinese-looking man also waiting there. Eventually we both came to the same conclusion that we were looking for each other. He told me he was a Kalmyk, from an ethnic minority of Mongol origin, with their own Republic in the north-east Caucasus. He was a friendly and intelligent man, who told me that diplomats in Russia's foreign service who came from the south and east of Russia were compelled to learn Far Eastern languages, and then served only in Far Eastern countries, which is why he was speaking fluent Vietnamese in Hanoi. We got on well and Christopher's talks went well. We then flew down to Danang, with its sandy beaches, its waving palm trees, and its MIG fighters in their bomb-proof hangars along the sides of the runway. We were shown the consulate building, which was quite modern, had about sixty rooms, a swimming pool, a tennis court and all mod cons. Perfect for a seaside hotel or business centre.

Three-way dialogue

We settled down for the talks. It is the only time in my life that I have done a three-way translation. "Good morning" said Christopher in English. "*Dobroye Utro*" I said in Russian to the lady concierge of the consulate, who was bilingual. "Good morning" she said in Vietnamese to the senior Vietnamese official present. "It is a pleasure to see you here," said the Vietnamese official. The lady passed this to me in Russian. I then passed it back to Christopher in English. It made for pretty slow progress, but it gave me a good deal of time to work out how best to say things. The Vietnamese official, who saw clearly that there might be a big cut for him if a Western business paid good money for a property on Vietnamese soil, took quite a shine to me. It was not easy to translate back to Christopher words to the effect of 'I like the look of your boy!'

Sad End

I do not know the outcome of the talks. Finance was well above my pay grade. And Christopher then appointed a Russian-speaking friend of mine to continue to conduct his negotiations *in situ,* and he became a sort of permanent representative in Vietnam. So that ended our relationship. But I was deeply shocked to hear what happened later, in November 2004. Christopher, 64, who had recently married his partner Angela Scott, was found dead with her in their luxury apartment in a 22-storey tower block in Monaco, the Sun Tower. Both had been shot, apparently with a handgun. She was on the bed and he was found, according to the papers, with a gun in his hand. One report said this was a 12-bore shotgun. A close friend of Christopher's said that he would never have owned a shotgun. Their bodies were discovered several weeks after their death. The Monaco police said it was suicide but I do not believe that. One online report wrote of 'some fanciful speculation of a Russian mafia connection'. It was reported that he was buying and selling property for wealthy Russians. An ex-Army friend of Christopher's, whom he spoke to on the phone twice a week, described him as 'a tremendous character, great fun, and a *bon viveur'*. It is a great mystery, and I am not aware of the case ever being solved.

Chapter 15: Sailing through Russia

One of my small ambitions was to cross Russia by water. It could be done by taking a trip by canal and river from Moscow to St Petersburg; and later taking a trip from Moscow round the 'Golden Circle' and down the Volga to Astrakhan, and then across to Rostov-on-Don. The last section had to be abandoned for some years, as the conflict in Eastern Ukraine made it rather dangerous, and after the Russian invasion, impossible. But I did manage in 2008, together with my wife Rosemary, to do the first part. I wrote about it for my fellow ex-naval interpreters of the Frinton Society. It was a trip designed for Western tourists. I have not changed anything. It reflects events of the time. Robert Avery, whom I refer to, is the former head of Russian at the Defence School of Languages.

Cruise boats moored at the Moscow River station. The one on the left is named after a People's Commissar for Foreign Affairs, the one on the right after an Old Bolshevik who Chairman of GosPlan.

You start – if you are with Noble Caledonia – at the Moscow River station. It was built by political prisoners in the Thirties. Lined up along a lengthy jetty are around a dozen boats, mostly named after obscure officials of the CPSU. But ours was named after the heroic poet, Sergei Yesenin. These all belong to MOSTURFLOT, and

CHAPTER FIFTEEN: SAILING THROUGH RUSSIA

you are in their hands for the ten day trip, which involves sleeping aboard for three nights in Moscow, six or seven days cruising along the Moscow canal, the Volga, the White Lake, Lake Ladoga, Lake Onega, and the Rivers Svir and Neva, and then four days in St Petersburg, with trips to Peterhof, Tsarskoye Selo and the Hermitage. First surprise is how many locks you have to go through to get down to sea level. And first tip: choose one of the smaller boats, so there are only Brits on it – one interpreter told me that on a large boat it took half an hour (because of multiple translations) just to introduce the captain. We had about seventy trippers, mostly older couples, but not without some interesting partnerships. You can sit with anyone at dinner (except for the 'toff table', who ate only with each other) and over the length of the trip you meet a wide range of types. The boat had a good range of English speaking receptionists, competent young female interpreters and a cheerful cruise director. When underway, there were lectures by a brilliant Russian professor, Ludmilla Selezneva, party games, vodka and blini parties, and a talent evening where trippers did everything from recite poetry to act out a Russian fairy story. I sang 'Kapitan' with Rosemary doing the actions! The rivers and canals were lined with birch trees, but occasionally you could see something unusual – a statue to old mother Volga, or a half-sunken bell tower, where Stalin had ordered whole villages to be inundated to create the Rybinsk reservoir for Moscow.

A large statue of Mother Volga

Just outside Moscow at Khimki there were two other unexpected sights: moored alongside some flats were an early 'Ekranoplan', a 'Tango' class submarine and a 'Krivak' class ASW frigate. Robert Avery tells me they are meant to be the beginnings of a naval

CHAPTER FIFTEEN: SAILING THROUGH RUSSIA

museum, which he has visited.

Krivak class frigate

The whole experience was very enjoyable and took us to places in the back of beyond like Uglich, Kirillov, Yaroslavl and Kizhi Island where there are enough icons, cupolas and painted boxes to satisfy the most demanding of cultural fanatics.

The all-wood Church of the Intercession on Kizhi Island, Lake Onega: watercolour

This was rural Russia, hardly changed from the thirties, where people lived in carved wooden shacks, had bath-houses by the river side, and still complained about the lack of agricultural equipment.

CHAPTER FIFTEEN: SAILING THROUGH RUSSIA

The historic tractor given to the Uglich farmers

At Uglich we were proudly shown the first tractor given to the village - unfortunately, said our guide, it was also the last! Off the beaten track old ladies were still begging, offering little posies of flowers, and at every landing stage there were stalls of every type of tourist trivia, from dolls and painted bowls to fur hats and redundant military kit. Living off tourists has become a major rural industry. Roads outside the big towns were still primitive – though in Moscow I was staggered to see how many cars there were on the streets, with traffic jams now an almost permanent feature. How I recall in the sixties those big wide urban roads, with only the odd army lorry to be seen, or a black limo purring up the centre VIP lane. I was also surprised by the wide availability now, not only of international consumer goods in the cities, but of good quality food in the provinces. In Yaroslavl, because of the rain, we went into an indoor food market – and it was teeming with fresh produce.

CHAPTER FIFTEEN: SAILING THROUGH RUSSIA

On Mandrogi Island, the old form of transport

On Mandrogi Island, a tourist trap on the Svir River, near St Petersburg, they were still using the old form of transport (above), though I wasn't sure whether this was just to be picturesque. Everywhere we went we were handed over to local guides who spoke with pride about Russia's history, its Royal family (special trip to the tombs of the Tsars) and its long cultural heritage. There were many churches to see, many icons to admire, many stories of Ivan the Terrible and Peter the Great to hear. In some churches and monasteries we were surprised by small a cappella choirs who sang religious chants and sacred music to entertain us Westerners. I found there was no longer that suspicion with which I have often been treated in the past – I was asked a number of times if I was a spy - they could not understand how I spoke Russian so fluently; eventually I tailored my reply into a joke: "No, I'm not – but I used to be!" That seemed to satisfy them – it half confirmed what they thought, while offering no threat. Mosturflot's crew were overwhelmingly friendly, from interpreters to waitresses to deck officers. The skipper even took me aside to ask what I really thought about all this business in Georgia. The trip was also an opportunity for me to do a lot of painting, and I end with this example, of the Church of St Elijah the Prophet in Yaroslavl on the Volga. (December 2008)

CHAPTER FIFTEEN: SAILING THROUGH RUSSIA

The Church of Elishah the Prophet at Yaroslavl: watercolour on a rainy day

Chapter 16: Conclusion

Our relations with the Russians have changed dramatically in 2022. Under Putin, with the invasion of Ukraine, they have become global lepers. But over the last seventy years those relations have varied considerably. The cold war, with a divided Germany and nuclear weapons in the hands of the US, the UK, France, and the USSR, was the spur to training Russian translators and interpreters in Britain. But we did not learn to hate Russians. We learned their language, we read their literature, we saw their ballet and their drama (for instance, in the late fifties I saw three plays by Chekhov at the Aldwych Theatre, performed in Russian by the Moscow State Arts Theatre) and on visits we made friends, if only briefly, with Russians. Up to the time of Gorbachev, relations could be chilly, as the leadership was rigidly Communist, and even speaking to foreigners was regarded with suspicion. But this gradually relaxed. And the Navy developed many warm and useful personal relationships through ship visits and conferences. The First Sea Lord, Sir Julian Oswald, who became the President of the Frinton Society, met many Soviet Admirals; he inspired their confidence, and developed excellent contacts. The Royal Navy has helped the Russian Navy, not only when the Russian submarine *Kursk* was lost, but also in Kamchatka in the Far East when the crew of a Russian submarine vessel was successfully rescued by British manpower and technology. But relations can turn from warm to frosty, and now it is going to take many years to return to an even keel. I have related the many different ways in which Russia and Russians have impacted on my life. I am sad that we are moving apart instead of moving back towards each other. But that is not possible just now. However I hope I have, in a small way, played a part in keeping relations friendly in difficult times.

CHAPTER SIXTEEN: CONCLUSION

Author on VE Day 2020

Bibliography and sources

Prof. Michael Lee *A Special Generation of Speakers of Russian* academic paper

Prof. Faith Wigzell : Paper for centenary of SSEES

Prof. Richard Vinen *National Service: Conscription in Britain 1945-1963* Allen Lane

Tony Cash and Mike Gerrard *The Coder Special Archive* pub. 2012

David Talks *Russian in My Life* My Saga

Brian Hawkins *Russian Language Training in the Services: A Personal memoir.*

I.W.Roberts *History of the School of Slavonic and East European Studies 1915 - 1990* SSEES Occasional Papers no. 14

BBC 'From our Own Correspondent'

Frinton Society 'Signals'

Photographs

All author's own except:

p.20, Tom Adams
http://www.caribbeanelections.com/knowledge/biography/bios/adams_tom.asp

p.22, Mausoleum: By Staron - Own work, CC BY-SA 3.0,
https://commons.wikimedia.org/w/index.php?curid=63418895

p.36, Sir Donald Insall,
https://www.donaldinsallassociates.co.uk/people/sir-donald-insall/

p.38, Sir Ian Trethowan
https://wiki.scotlandonair.com/w/images/6/69/1977_Ian_Trethowan.jpg

p.45, Gerald Carroll *Internet*

p.51, Metropole, Hanoi (now called Sofitel Legend Metropole)
https://www.sofitel-legend-metropole-hanoi.com/

Printed in Great Britain
by Amazon